DO MATH WITH SPORTS STATS!

HOCKEY

Stats, Facts, and Figures

BY KATE MIKOLEY

Gareth Stevens
PUBLISHING

Please visit our website, www.garethstevens.com. For a free color catalog of all our high-quality books, call toll free 1-800-542-2595 or fax 1-877-542-2596.

Cataloging-in-Publication Data

Names: Mikoley, Kate.
Title: Hockey: stats, facts, and figures / Kate Mikoley.
Description: New York : Gareth Stevens Publishing, 2018. | Series: Do math with sports stats! | Includes index.
Identifiers: LCCN ISBN 9781538211373 (pbk.) | ISBN 9781538211397 (library bound) | ISBN 9781538211380 (6 pack)
Subjects: LCSH: Hockey–Mathematics–Juvenile literature. | Hockey–Statistics–Juvenile literature. | Hockey–Juvenile literature.
Classification: LCC GV847.25 M47 2018 | DDC 796.9620151–dc23

First Edition

Published in 2018 by
Gareth Stevens Publishing
111 East 14th Street, Suite 349
New York, NY 10003

Copyright © 2018 Gareth Stevens Publishing

Designer: Samantha DeMartin
Editor: Kate Mikoley

Photo credits: pp. 4–29 (paperclips) AVS-Images/Shutterstock.com; covers, pp. 1–29 (pencil) irin-k/Shutterstock.com; pp. 4–29 (post-its) Pixel Embargo/Shutterstock.com; pp. 4–29 (tape) Flas100/Shutterstock.com; pp. 3–32 (graph paper) BLACKDAY/Shutterstock.com; covers, pp. 1–32 (bleacher texture) Al Sermeno Photography/Shutterstock.com; covers, pp. 1–29 (clipboard) Mega Pixel/Shutterstock.com; covers, pp. 1–29 (formula overlay) lolya1988/Shutterstock.com; covers, pp. 1–29 (index card) photastic/Shutterstock.com; cover, p. 1 Fotokvadrat/Shutterstock.com; pp. 5, 23 Icon Sportswire/Icon Sportswire/Getty Images; p. 6 Alex Goykhman/Wikimedia Commons; p. 7 B Bennett/Bruce Bennett/Getty Images; p. 8 Bardocz Peter/Shutterstock.com; p. 9 Adam Vilimek/Shutterstock.com; p. 10 Steve Babineau/National Hockey League/Getty Images; p. 11 Jim McIsaac/Getty Images Sport/Getty Images; pp. 13, 21, 27 (top) Bruce Bennett/Getty Images Sport/Getty Images; p. 14 Joe Sargent/National Hockey League/Getty Images; p. 15 Jared Silber/National Hockey League/Getty Images; p. 17 V Pugliese/Bruce Bennett/Getty Images; p. 18 Grushin/Shutterstock.com; p. 19 Debora Robinson/National Hockey League/Getty Images; p. 22 Christian Petersen/Getty Images Sport/Getty Images; p. 24 Patrick Smith/Getty Images Sport/Getty Images; p. 25 Jonathan Daniel/Getty Images Sport/Getty Images; p. 27 (bottom) Kirk Irwin/Getty Images Sport/Getty Images; p. 29 Len Redkoles/National Hockey League/Getty Images.

Printed in the United States of America

CPSIA compliance information: Batch #CW18GS: For further information contact Gareth Stevens, New York, New York at 1-800-542-2595.

CONTENTS

Words in the glossary appear in **bold** type the first time they are used in the text.

ON THE ICE

Gliding toward the visiting team's net, a hockey player on the home team guides the puck. Ducking away from his **opponent**, he uses his stick to pass the puck to his teammate. Within seconds, the teammate shoots the puck toward the net. The goalie tries to make the save, but misses. The home team scores!

Hockey is a popular sport all over the world. In the United States and Canada, ice hockey is one of the most popular **professional** sports. From the time on the clock to the score on the board, numbers and math play a huge part in this game!

KNOW YOUR NUMBERS

The object of the game is to score the most goals, but those aren't the only numbers that matter in hockey! Statistics, or stats, are numbers that show how well a team or player is doing at a certain skill or part of the game.

STATS KEEP TRACK OF
GAME PLAY, SUCH AS GOALS,
THROUGHOUT GAMES,
WHOLE SEASONS, AND EVEN
A PLAYER'S WHOLE CAREER!

In 1875, the first known public indoor ice hockey game was played in Canada between two teams of college students. By the late 1800s, hockey was one of Canada's most popular sports and soon spread to the United States. In 1903, the first recognized professional hockey team—the Portage Lakers—was formed in Michigan. A year later, a professional league was formed.

THE CHAMPIONSHIPS

Every year, the winner of the NHL championship receives the Stanley Cup. This is the oldest trophy for pro athletes in North America, first given in 1893. A Canadian official, Lord Stanley of Preston, originally **donated** the cup to be given to the top Canadian team. The cup has been in the NHL since 1926.

the Stanley Cup

In 1917, the National Hockey League (NHL) was formed. Now the major professional hockey league of North America, the NHL was originally made up of five Canadian teams. In 1924, the first US team joined the NHL.

THE MONTREAL **AMATEUR** ATHLETIC ASSOCIATION TEAM WAS THE FIRST TO WIN THE STANLEY CUP!

An ice hockey rink usually looks like a rectangle with rounded corners. In the NHL, rinks are 200 feet (60 m) by 85 feet (26 m). There is a goal, or net, near each end of the rink, with a goal line marked on the ice at the front of the net. A curved line in front of the net is called the crease.

Two blue lines separate the rink into three parts. The middle part of the rink between the two blue lines is called the **neutral** zone. The neutral zone is divided in half by the red center line.

KNOW THE RINK

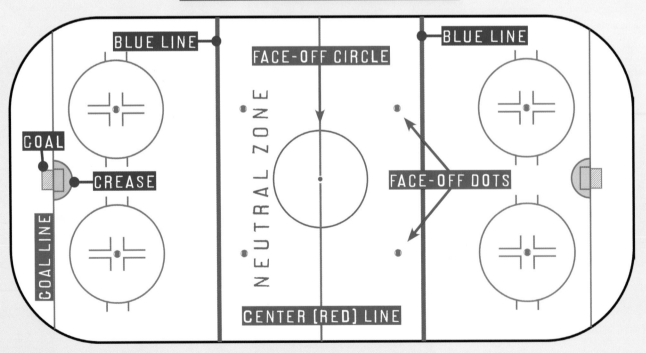

BLUE LINE
FACE-OFF CIRCLE
BLUE LINE
GOAL
CREASE
NEUTRAL ZONE
FACE-OFF DOTS
GOAL LINE
CENTER (RED) LINE

THERE ARE NINE DOTS ON THE ICE WHERE **FACE-OFFS** HAPPEN. CIRCLES SURROUND FIVE OF THESE DOTS. ONLY THE TWO PLAYERS IN THE FACE-OFF ARE ALLOWED IN THESE CIRCLES.

THE NUMBERS GAME

THE BLUE LINES ARE USUALLY 25 FEET FROM THE CENTER LINE, MAKING THE NEUTRAL ZONE 50 FEET WIDE. THE LENGTH OF THIS ZONE IS THE SAME AS THE WIDTH OF THE RINK, 85 FEET. WHAT'S THE AREA OF THE NEUTRAL ZONE? REMEMBER, THE AREA OF A RECTANGLE IS THE LENGTH TIMES THE WIDTH. ANSWER ON PAGE 29.

FILLING THE ROSTER

Each team usually has six players on the rink at a time, including the goalie. The other five players usually include three forwards and two **defensemen**. The three forward positions are center, left wing, and right wing.

HOCKEY IS THE ONLY MAJOR SPORT WHERE **SUBSTITUTIONS** HAPPEN WHILE THE GAME IS STILL BEING **PLAYED**, RATHER THAN WHEN THE CLOCK IS STOPPED.

While a team only has six players on the ice at a time, there are many more on the bench waiting to be put in the game. Hockey is a game that moves quickly, and the players on the ice change often. Forwards usually only play for 90 seconds at a time! In the NHL, a team can "dress," or play, 20 players from their **roster** in a game.

forward John Tavares

THE NUMBERS GAME

A STANDARD NHL GAME HAS 60 MINUTES OF PLAYING TIME. THIS IS DIVIDED INTO THREE PERIODS, EACH 20 MINUTES LONG. LET'S SAY A PLAYER PLAYED A TOTAL OF 24 MINUTES IN A GAME. OF THIS TIME, 1/4 WAS PLAYED IN THE FIRST PERIOD. HOW MANY MINUTES DID THE PLAYER PLAY IN THE FIRST PERIOD?

ANSWER ON PAGE 29.

$$24 \times \frac{1}{4}$$

FACING OFF

Hockey games begin with a face-off. This is when an official drops the puck between one player from each team. The players each try to help their team gain control of the puck. Face-offs are used throughout the game to restart play when it has stopped. At the beginning of the game, the face-off happens at the center of the ice, but later, face-offs can happen on any of the nine face-off dots.

Face-off percentage is a stat used in hockey that shows the rate a player wins face-offs. It takes into account the total face-offs they've taken part in and number that they've won.

THE NUMBERS GAME

SOME CENTERS TAKE PART IN MORE THAN 1,000 FACE-OFFS THROUGHOUT THE 82-GAME SEASON. LET'S SAY A PLAYER TOOK PART IN 1,208 FACE-OFFS. IF THEY LOST 603 OF THESE FACE-OFFS, HOW MANY OF THEM DID THEY WIN?

ANSWER ON PAGE 29.

THE PLAYERS WHO TAKE PART IN FACE-OFFS ARE USUALLY CENTERS, ALTHOUGH SOMETIMES OTHER PLAYERS DO SO, TOO. HERE, KELLI STACK OF THE US WOMEN'S NATIONAL HOCKEY TEAM AND HAYLEY WICKENHEISER OF CANADA'S NATIONAL WOMEN'S HOCKEY TEAM FACE OFF IN THE 2014 WINTER OLYMPICS.

GETTING THE GOAL

Forwards are the players who most often try to make goals. They do this by shooting the puck toward the other team's net as much as possible. It's the defensemen's job to try to keep the puck from coming near their team's goalie. When the puck does get close to the net, it's the goalie's job to keep it from going into the net.

Sidney Crosby

IN THE 2016-2017 NHL SEASON, SIDNEY CROSBY PLAYED 75 GAMES WITH THE PITTSBURGH PENGUINS AND SCORED 44 GOALS. THAT WAS THE MOST GOALS ANY PLAYER SCORED THAT SEASON!

The way a hockey team wins a game is by scoring more goals than the other team. Because of this, many people would say goals are the most important stat of all in hockey. Each goal is worth one point.

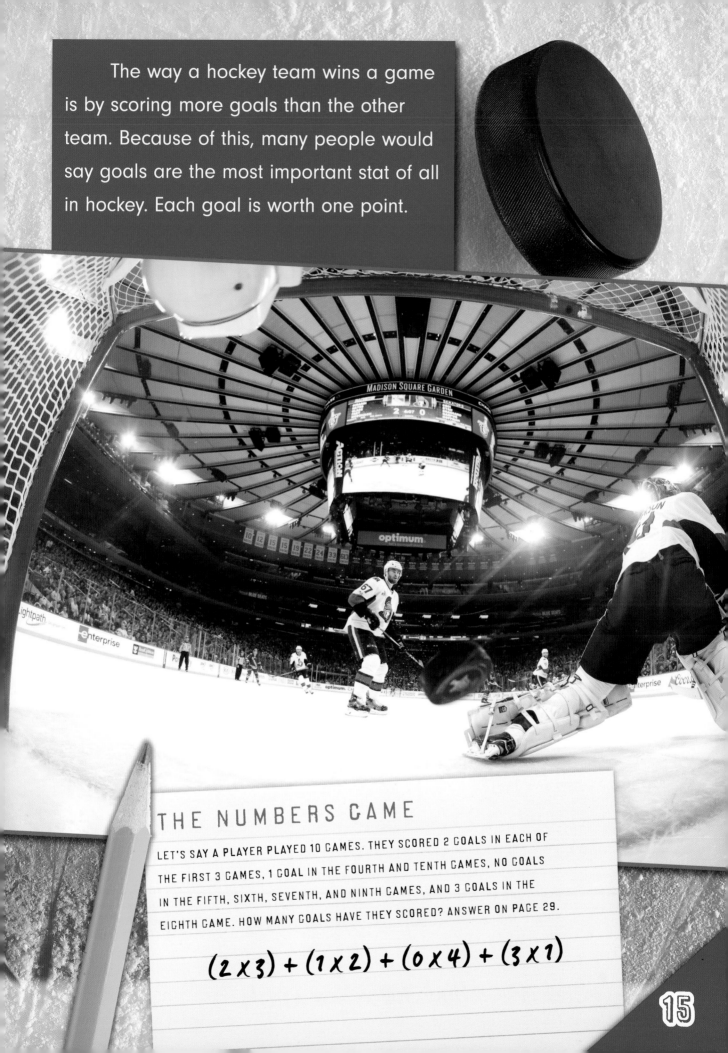

THE NUMBERS GAME

LET'S SAY A PLAYER PLAYED 10 GAMES. THEY SCORED 2 GOALS IN EACH OF THE FIRST 3 GAMES, 1 GOAL IN THE FOURTH AND TENTH GAMES, NO GOALS IN THE FIFTH, SIXTH, SEVENTH, AND NINTH GAMES, AND 3 GOALS IN THE EIGHTH GAME. HOW MANY GOALS HAVE THEY SCORED? ANSWER ON PAGE 29.

$$(2 \times 3) + (1 \times 2) + (0 \times 4) + (3 \times 1)$$

WHAT'S THE POINT?

Hockey players can also get recognized for a point even if they aren't the one to make the goal. This happens when they make an assist. This is when a player on the scoring team contributes to the goal, but isn't the one to make the goal. This can happen by passing, shooting, or **deflecting** the puck. For each goal, an assist is given to up to two players who touched the puck before the goal was scored and helped make it happen.

Sometimes goals are considered unassisted. This happens if a team loses possession of the puck to a player who scores without any other teammates touching the puck.

THE NUMBERS GAME

STATS ARE KEPT FOR BOTH GOALS AND ASSISTS. EACH IS WORTH ONE POINT TOWARD A PLAYER'S STATS. THE STAT THAT SHOWS A PLAYER'S COMBINED GOALS AND ASSISTS IS CALLED POINTS. LET'S SAY A PLAYER HAS 108 POINTS. IF 2/3 OF THESE POINTS ARE FROM ASSISTS, HOW MANY GOALS DID THE PLAYER MAKE? ANSWER ON PAGE 29.

Hint: $108 \times \dfrac{2}{3} = assists$

WAYNE GRETZKY PLAYED IN THE NHL FROM 1979 TO 1999. OVER THE COURSE OF HIS NHL CAREER, HE HAD 2,857 POINTS! HE WAS SO GOOD THAT HE WAS NICKNAMED THE "GREAT ONE."

Points are important, but they don't show everything. Two players might be about the same skill level, but one who played fewer games would probably have fewer points. One player may have played for 10 years and another for only 5. If the player who's played for 10 years has more points, it doesn't necessarily mean they're better than the player who's only played for 5 years.

Points per game allows people to compare players who've played a different number of games. To **calculate** points per game, you divide the total number of points a player has by the number of games they've played.

BREAKING DOWN THE POINTS

In the NHL, each team plays 82 games in the regular season. If a player plays all 82 games and gets a total of 82 points, that would be an average of 1.00 point per game. In the 2016–2017 season, only 9 players in the NHL had a points-per-game average higher than 1.00!

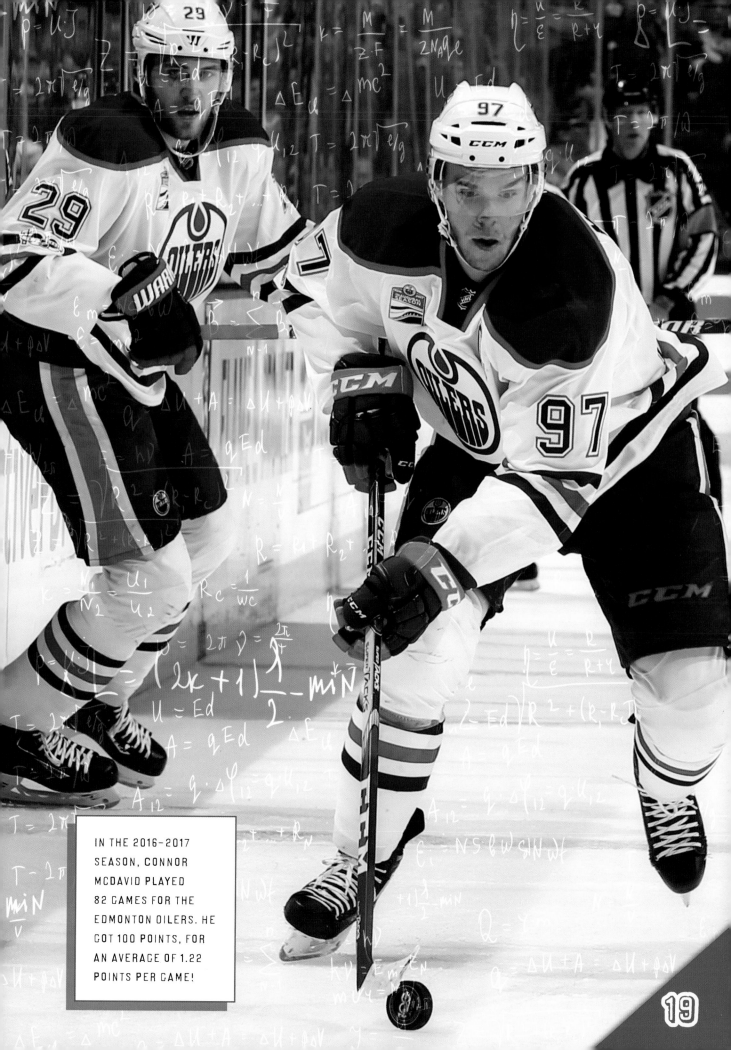

IN THE 2016-2017 SEASON, CONNOR MCDAVID PLAYED 82 GAMES FOR THE EDMONTON OILERS. HE GOT 100 POINTS, FOR AN AVERAGE OF 1.22 POINTS PER GAME!

PENALTIES AND POWER PLAYS

Though they start off with six players, a team doesn't always get to keep their players on the ice. Penalties, or punishments for breaking a rule, happen fairly regularly in hockey. When a player commits a penalty, they often have to sit out for a certain amount of time in the penalty box. Their team continues playing without subbing in another player. When one team has more players on the ice, it's called a power play.

Most penalties are minor penalties and result in the player sitting out for 2 minutes. The player can come back if the other team scores or after the time is up.

THE NUMBERS GAME

MORE SERIOUS PENALTIES RECEIVE A LONGER TIME IN THE PENALTY BOX OR CAN EVEN GET A PLAYER KICKED OUT OF THE GAME. PENALTIES IN MINUTES TRACKS A PLAYER'S PENALTY TIME. IF A PLAYER SPENT 600 SECONDS IN THE PENALTY BOX, HOW MANY MINUTES WERE THEY OUT OF THE GAME FOR? REMEMBER, THERE ARE 60 SECONDS IN A MINUTE. ANSWER ON PAGE 29.

Matt Martin sits in the penalty box.

Goalies can commit penalties, too. When this happens, another member of the team sits out so the goalie can stay in the game during the power play. The team with more players on the ice has the advantage. This is often a good opportunity to score because there are fewer players around to block the shot. Special stats help measure how well a team or player performs during power plays.

Any time a team scores while they have more players on the ice, it's considered a power play goal. A team's power play percentage shows how often they score during power play opportunities.

POWER PLAY PERCENTAGE IS SOMETIMES ALSO REFERRED TO AS THE POWER PLAY CONVERSION RATE. THIS IS BECAUSE IT SHOWS THE RATE AT WHICH A TEAM CONVERTS POWER PLAY OPPORTUNITIES INTO GOALS.

Marcus Foligno sets up during a power play.

THE NUMBERS GAME

IN THE 2016-2017 NHL SEASON, THE BUFFALO SABRES HAD THE HIGHEST POWER PLAY PERCENTAGE. IN 233 POWER PLAY OPPORTUNITIES, THEY SCORED 57 GOALS, GIVING THEM A POWER PLAY PERCENTAGE OF 24.5. HOW MANY FACTORS ARE IN THE NUMBER 57? WHAT ARE THEY? REMEMBER, FACTORS ARE NUMBERS YOU CAN MULTIPLY TOGETHER TO GET ANOTHER NUMBER. ANSWER ON PAGE 29.

PLUS OR MINUS?

If the team with fewer players on the ice scores, it's called a shorthanded goal. When both teams have the same number of players on the ice, a goal is considered an even-strength goal. Plus-minus is a stat that keeps track of these goals on the individual level.

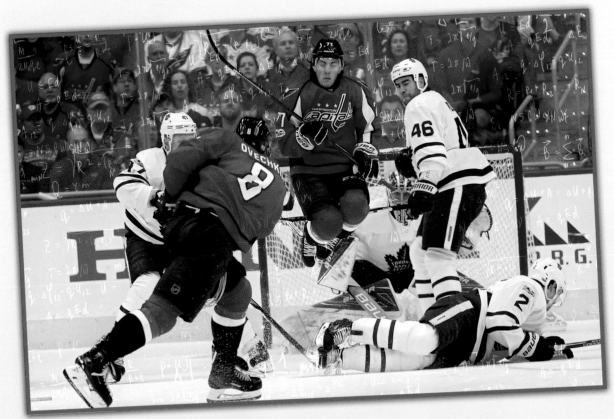

Alex Ovechkin shoots for a goal.

A player gets a "plus" if they're on the ice when their team scores an even-strength or shorthanded goal. If they're on the ice when the other team does this, they get a "minus." The difference is the player's plus-minus. Some think a higher plus-minus is the sign of a strong player, but many others think plus-minus isn't a dependable stat.

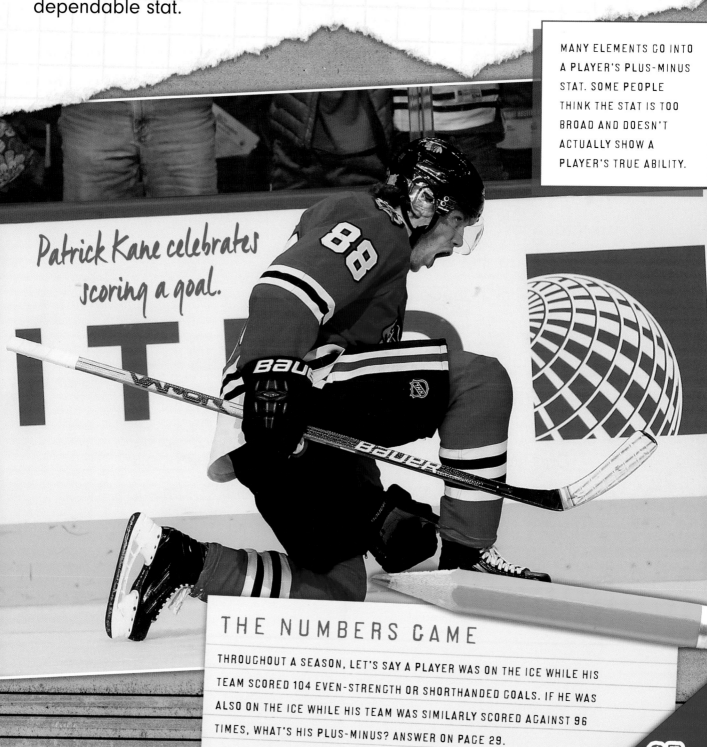

Patrick Kane celebrates scoring a goal.

MANY ELEMENTS GO INTO A PLAYER'S PLUS-MINUS STAT. SOME PEOPLE THINK THE STAT IS TOO BROAD AND DOESN'T ACTUALLY SHOW A PLAYER'S TRUE ABILITY.

THE NUMBERS GAME

THROUGHOUT A SEASON, LET'S SAY A PLAYER WAS ON THE ICE WHILE HIS TEAM SCORED 104 EVEN-STRENGTH OR SHORTHANDED GOALS. IF HE WAS ALSO ON THE ICE WHILE HIS TEAM WAS SIMILARLY SCORED AGAINST 96 TIMES, WHAT'S HIS PLUS-MINUS? ANSWER ON PAGE 29.

BLOCKING THE GOAL

Great hockey teams need great players for all positions, but there's only one player who will often stay on the ice throughout the entire game—the goalie! Goalies block the puck from going in the net. While most players sub in and out of the game very often, the goalie commonly plays the entire 60 minutes.

A TEAM EFFORT

Goalies want to have a low GAA. A high GAA could mean a goalie is not very good, but not always. The goalie's defensive teammates play a part in his GAA. If they let a lot of goals reach him, his GAA may be higher. Likewise, if they block a lot of shots, it will likely be lower.

One stat that shows a goalie's ability is their goals against average (GAA). To figure this stat out, you multiply the number of goals a goalie has allowed, or let in the net, by 60. You then divide that number by the number of minutes the goalie has played.

BRADEN HOLTBY OF THE WASHINGTON CAPITALS AND SERGEI BOBROVSKY OF THE COLUMBUS BLUE JACKETS BOTH ALLOWED 127 GOALS IN THE 2016–2017 SEASON. BUT BOBROVSKY PLAYED MORE MINUTES, GIVING HIM A GAA 0.01 LOWER THAN HOLTBY!

Braden Holtby

Sergei Bobrovsky

Math can help you figure out different hockey stats. It can also help you score while you're on the ice! Angles can play an important part in helping make a goal. Imagine two lines coming from either end of the goal and meeting at the puck. That's the shooting angle. The wider the angle, the easier it is to score. The goalie can block a player's angle, so passing is extremely important.

Teamwork is a big part of hockey. A player can have the best stats, but in the end, most stats aren't what win the game. Teams that work well together often do the best.

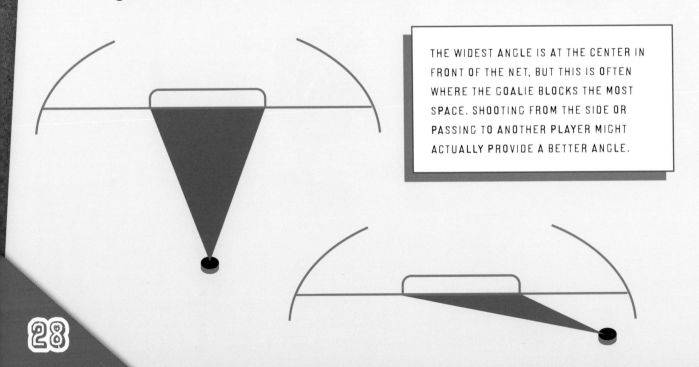

THE WIDEST ANGLE IS AT THE CENTER IN FRONT OF THE NET, BUT THIS IS OFTEN WHERE THE GOALIE BLOCKS THE MOST SPACE. SHOOTING FROM THE SIDE OR PASSING TO ANOTHER PLAYER MIGHT ACTUALLY PROVIDE A BETTER ANGLE.

ANSWER KEY

p. 9 – 4,250 square feet

p. 11 – 6 minutes

p. 12 – 605

p. 15 – 11 goals

p. 16 – 36 goals

p. 20 – 10 minutes

p. 23 – 4 factors; 1, 3, 19, 57

p. 25 – 8

THE SLAP SHOT

Hockey is a game of speed, but it's not just the players that dart around. The puck sometimes reaches speeds of more than 100 miles (161 km) per hour! The fastest shot in hockey is the slap shot. This is when a player lifts their stick backwards from the ice and brings it forward to "slap" the puck.

GLOSSARY

amateur: someone who does something without pay

calculate: to figure something out using math

defenseman: a player skilled at stopping other players from scoring

deflect: to cause something that is moving to change direction

donate: to give something

face-off: a method of beginning play by dropping the puck between two players

neutral: not belonging to or favoring either side in a contest

opponent: the person or team you must beat to win a game

professional: earning money from an activity that many people do for fun

roster: the list of people who are on a team

substitution: the act of replacing one player with another

FOR MORE INFORMATION

BOOKS

Kortemeier, Todd. *Pro Hockey by the Numbers*. North Mankato, MN: Capstone Press, 2016.

Mahaney, Ian F. *The Math of Hockey*. New York, NY: PowerKids Press, 2011.

WEBSITES

Hockey Can Help You Meet Your Future Goals

futuregoals.nhl.com/future-goals-stem-module

Can you answer these hockey questions? Your math skills will help you figure out some of them!

Statistics

www.espn.com/nhl/statistics

Stay up to date with the stats of your favorite teams and players here.

Publisher's note to educators and parents: Our editors have carefully reviewed these websites to ensure that they are suitable for students. Many websites change frequently, however, and we cannot guarantee that a site's future contents will continue to meet our high standards of quality and educational value. Be advised that students should be closely supervised whenever they access the Internet.

INDEX